TITLE OF YOUR TRIP..

GET READY TO BECOME A STORY TELLER...

ADVENTURE YEARLY OVERVIEW

TRIPS TO PLAN & WHEN

Jan	Feb	Mar

Apr	May	Jun

Jul	Aug	Sep

Oct	Nov	Dec

INITIAL IDEAS

JOT ALL OF YOUR IDEAS, PLANS AND VISIONS FOR THE TRIP HERE

PLACES TO VISIT/ATTRACTIONS
(MUST SEE/DO EXPERIENCES I.E. HIKES/TRAILS, RESTAURANT, BEACHES/LAKES, EXCURSIONS)

PLACES TO VISIT	LOCATION	WHEN

PLACES TO VISIT	LOCATION	WHEN

PLACES TO VISIT/ATTRACTIONS

(MUST SEE/DO EXPERIENCES I.E. HIKES/TRAILS, RESTAURANT, BEACHES/LAKES, EXCURSIONS)

PLACES TO VISIT	LOCATION	WHEN

PLACES TO VISIT	LOCATION	WHEN

ITINERARY & PLANS

ACTIVITIES/PLANS	DATES	TIMES

ITINERARY & PLANS

ACTIVITIES/PLANS	DATES	TIMES

MONTHLY OVERVIEW

NOTE HERE KEY DATE REMINDERS FOR TRAVEL DATES, WHERE YOU WILL BE, APPOINTMENTS, DESTINATION STOPS ETC

MONTH: _____

MON	TUE	WED	THU	FRI	SAT	SUN

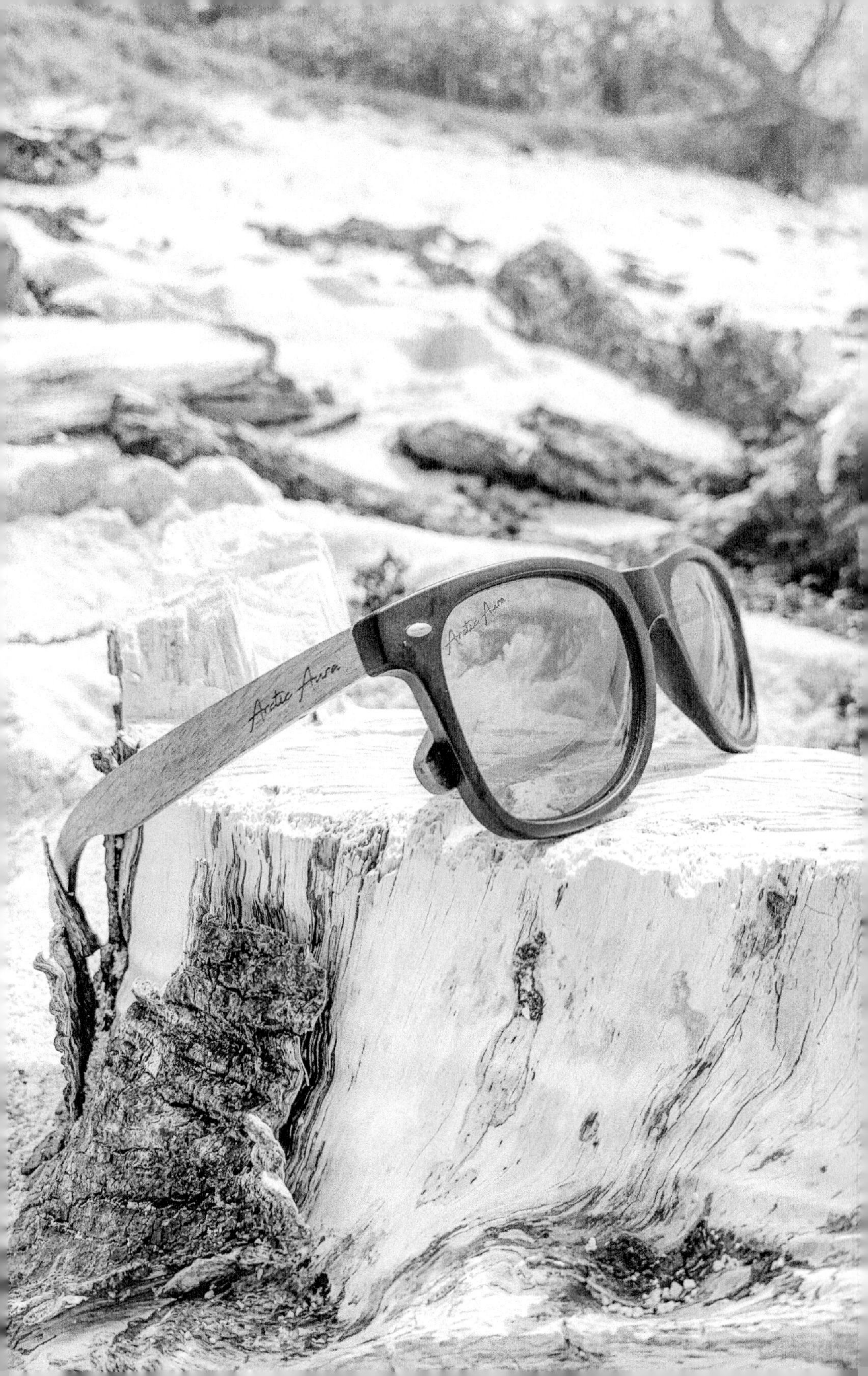
Arctic Aura
Arctic Aura

BUDGET PLANNING

ALLOCATE HOW MUCH MONEY YOU'LL NEED FOR EACH

PROVISIONS

FOOD	DRINKS	EATING OUT

BEING A TOURIST

EXCURSIONS	TRANSPORT	DINNER

TRAVEL

MISCELLANEOUS	FUEL	HIRE CAR

OTHER

SPENDING MONEY	MISCELLANEOUS	EMERGENCY

SAVINGS TRACKER

SAVING FOR: _____

GOAL AMOUNT: _____   DEADLINE: _____

DETAILS OF MONEY SAVED	AMOUNT	TOTAL SAVED

GETTING ORGANISED – PACKING

WHAT TO PACK

CLOTHES

ACCESSORIES

SPECIALIST EQUIPMENT

FOOD/SUPPLIES

GETTING ORGANISED
– ENTERTAINMENT

TRAVEL & RECREATIONAL ENTERTAINMENT

PLAYLISTS

PODCASTS

BOOKS & READING MATERIALS

CONSOLES/TECHNOLOGY ELECTRONICS

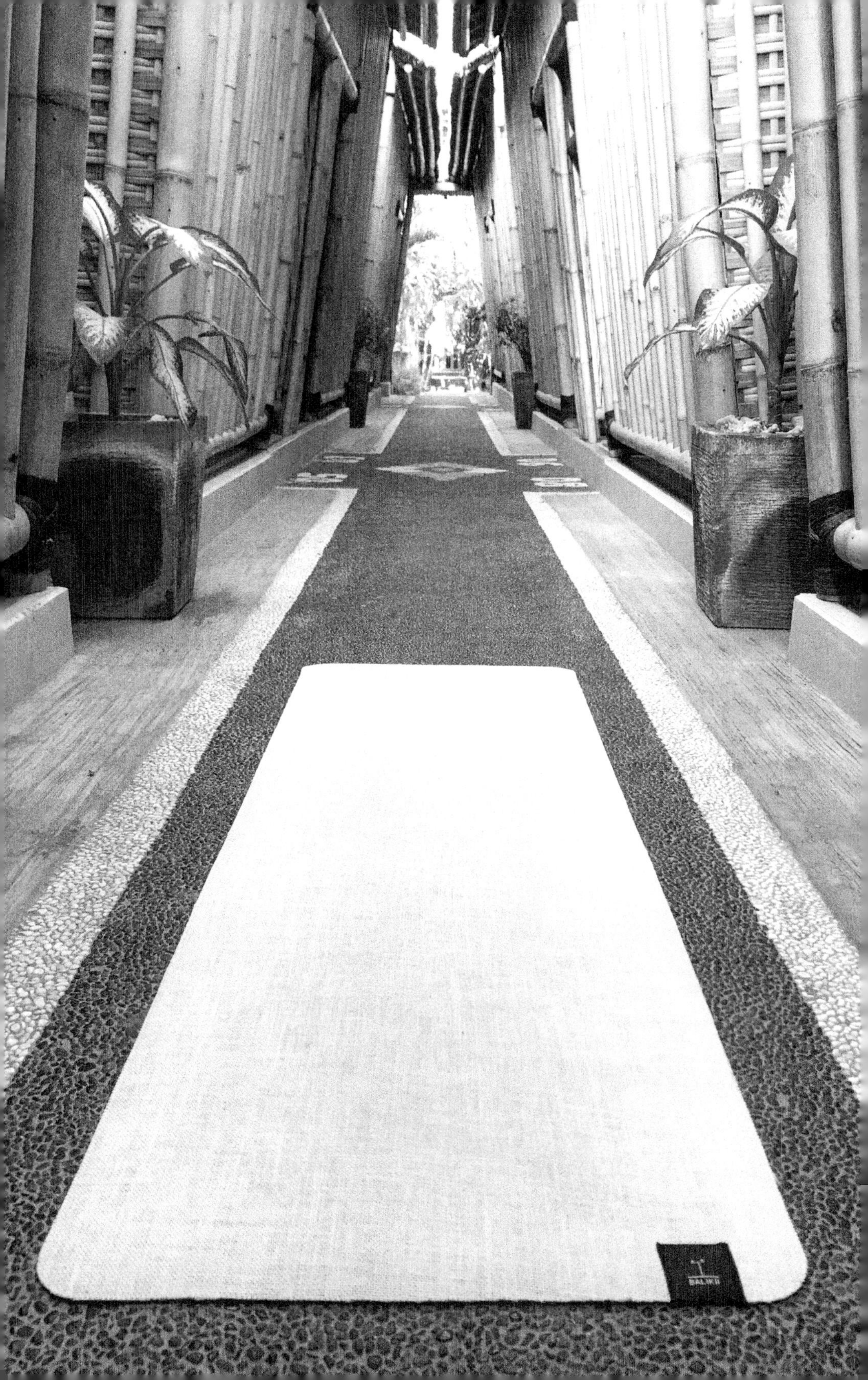

ACCOMMODATION

NAME OF ACCOMMODATION:

ADDRESS	LENGTH OF STAY	SCORE OUT OF 10

REVIEW/EXPERIENCE OF STAY

STAY AGAIN? ☐ YES ☐ NO

NAME OF ACCOMMODATION:

ADDRESS	LENGTH OF STAY	SCORE OUT OF 10

REVIEW/EXPERIENCE OF STAY

STAY AGAIN? ☐ YES ☐ NO

ACCOMMODATION

NAME OF ACCOMMODATION:

| ADDRESS | LENGTH OF STAY | SCORE OUT OF 10 |

REVIEW/EXPERIENCE OF STAY

STAY AGAIN?   ☐ YES   ☐ NO

NAME OF ACCOMMODATION:

| ADDRESS | LENGTH OF STAY | SCORE OUT OF 10 |

REVIEW/EXPERIENCE OF STAY

STAY AGAIN?   ☐ YES   ☐ NO

TRIP BUDGET TRACKER

BUDGET TOTAL

MONEY SPENT ON	AMOUNT	REMAINING

TRIP BUDGET TRACKER

CARRIED OVER

MONEY SPENT ON	AMOUNT	REMAINING

LOCAL BUSINESSES

NAME OF BUSINESS:		
ADDRESS	CONTACT NO	DETAILS

NAME OF BUSINESS:		
ADDRESS	CONTACT NO	DETAILS

NAME OF BUSINESS:		
ADDRESS	CONTACT NO	DETAILS

NAME OF BUSINESS:		
ADDRESS	CONTACT NO	DETAILS

LOCAL BUSINESSES

NAME OF BUSINESS:
ADDRESS	CONTACT NO	DETAILS

NAME OF BUSINESS:
ADDRESS	CONTACT NO	DETAILS

NAME OF BUSINESS:
ADDRESS	CONTACT NO	DETAILS

NAME OF BUSINESS:
ADDRESS	CONTACT NO	DETAILS

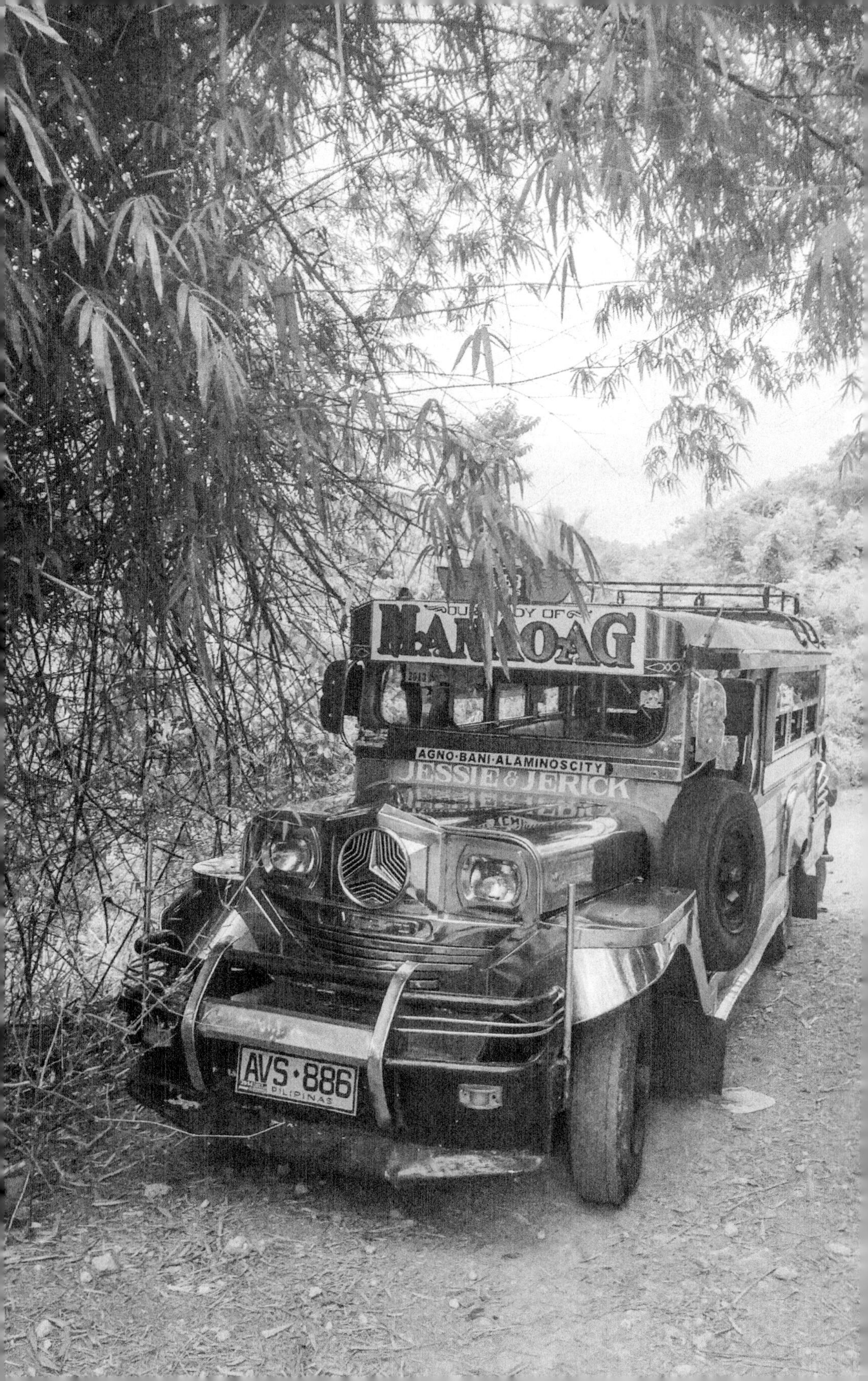
AGNO·BANI·ALAMINOSCITY
JESSIE & JERICK
AVS·886
PILIPINAS

TRAVEL & TRANSPORT

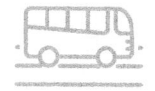

| MODES OF TRANSPORT | DATES | TIMES |

TRAVEL & TRANSPORT

MODES OF TRANSPORT **DATES** **TIMES**

OTHER IMPORTANT TRAVEL INFO & ROUTE MAPPING

JOURNEYS & ROUTES

TRAVEL INFO & ROUTE MAPPING

TRAVEL INFO & ROUTE MAPPING

DOODLES, DRAWINGS & IDEAS

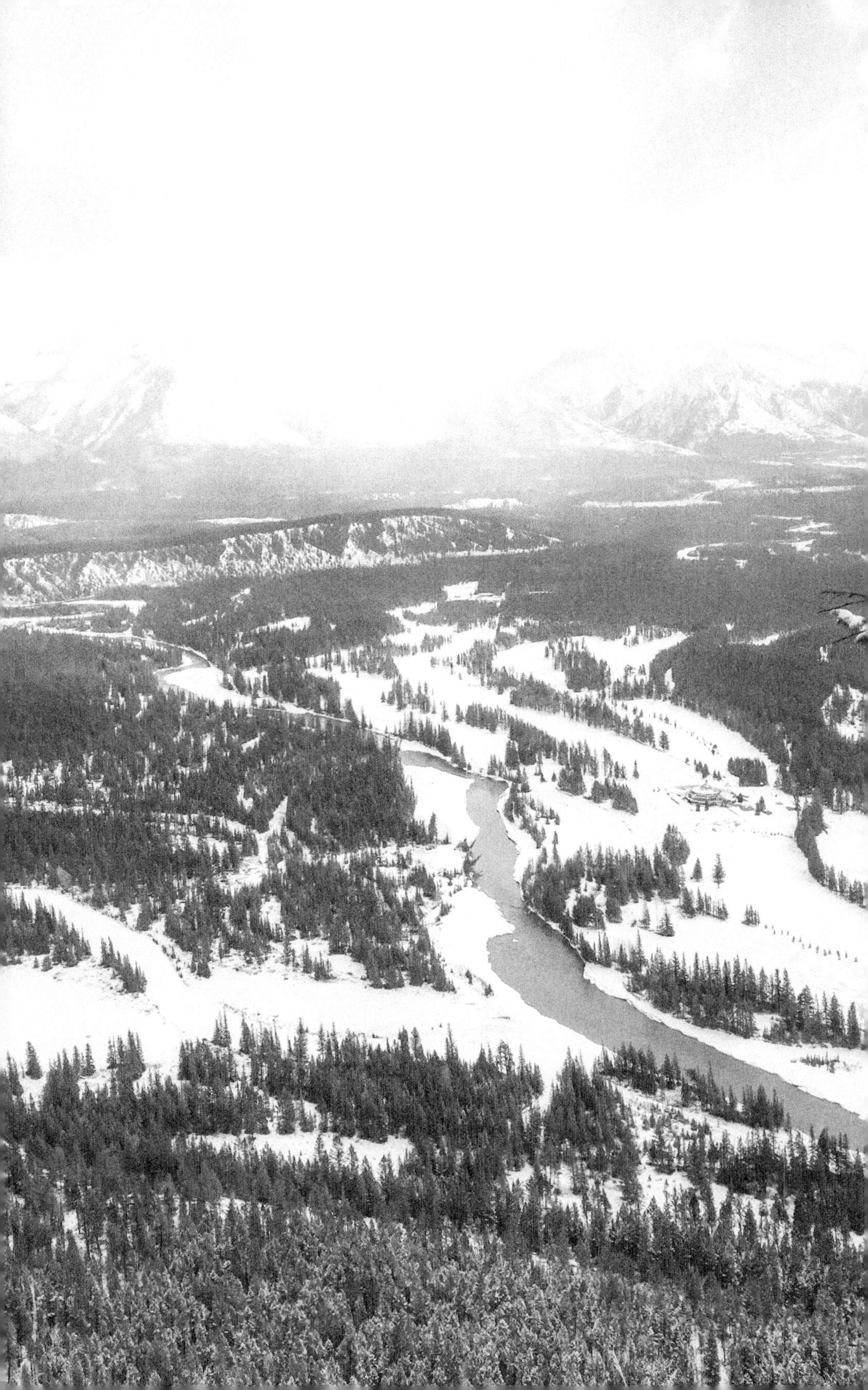

MEMORIES – PLACES VISITED

DESTINATION:

WHAT I SAW, ATE, FELT, EXPERIENCED, PEOPLE MET

FUNNY OR KEY MOMENTS TO REMEMBER

WHAT I'LL TAKE AWAY FROM THE EXPERIENCE

JOURNAL

MEMORIES - PLACES VISITED

DESTINATION:

WHAT I SAW, ATE, FELT, EXPERIENCED, PEOPLE MET

FUNNY OR KEY MOMENTS TO REMEMBER

WHAT I'LL TAKE AWAY FROM THE EXPERIENCE

JOURNAL

MEMORIES - PLACES VISITED

DESTINATION:

WHAT I SAW, ATE, FELT, EXPERIENCED, PEOPLE MET

FUNNY OR KEY MOMENTS TO REMEMBER

WHAT I'LL TAKE AWAY FROM THE EXPERIENCE

JOURNAL

MEMORIES - PLACES VISITED

DESTINATION:

WHAT I SAW, ATE, FELT, EXPERIENCED, PEOPLE MET

FUNNY OR KEY MOMENTS TO REMEMBER

WHAT I'LL TAKE AWAY FROM THE EXPERIENCE

JOURNAL

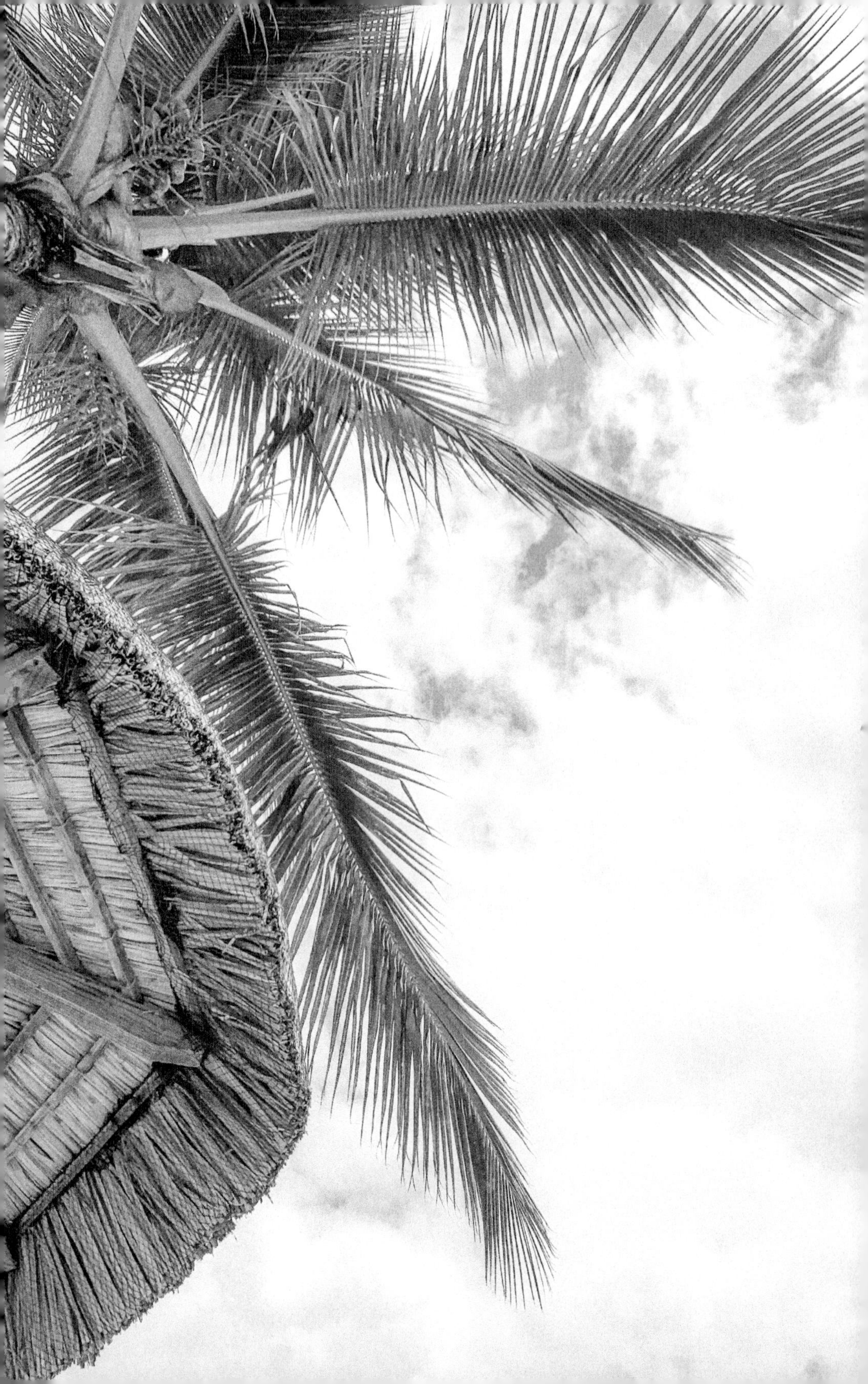

PLACE YOUR MEMORIES

STICK PHOTOS, TICKETS, MAPS

PLACE YOUR MEMORIES

STICK PHOTOS, TICKETS, MAPS

PLACE YOUR MEMORIES

STICK PHOTOS, TICKETS, MAPS

PLACE YOUR MEMORIES

STICK PHOTOS, TICKETS, MAPS

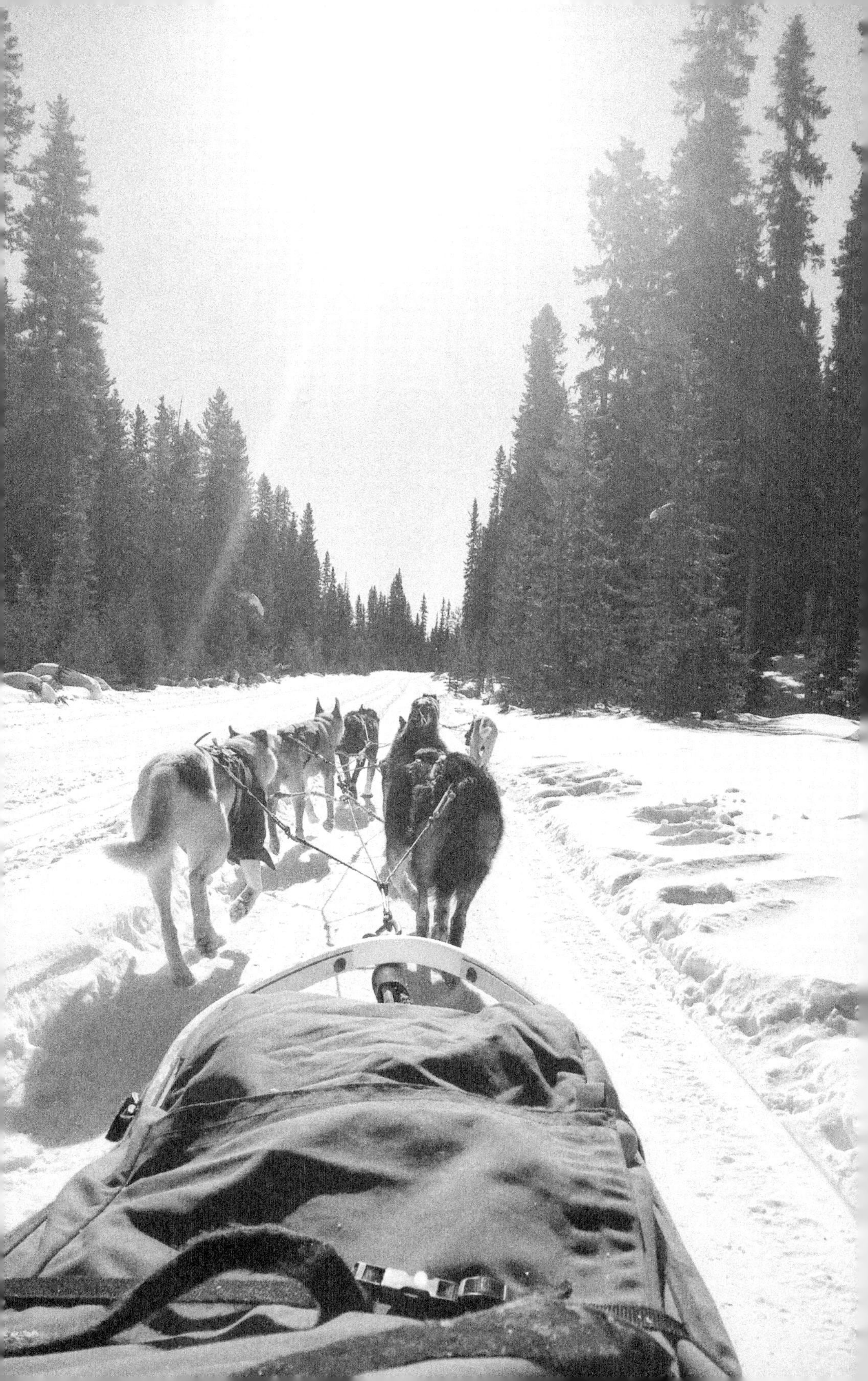

REFLECTION

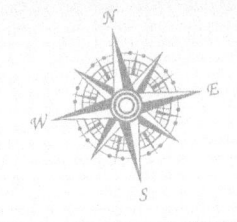

WHAT I'D DO DIFFERENTLY NEXT TIME

THINGS I'VE LEARNT

ADVICE I'D GIVE TO OTHERS

NOTES

NOTES

NOTES

NOTES

NOTES

NOTES

NOTES

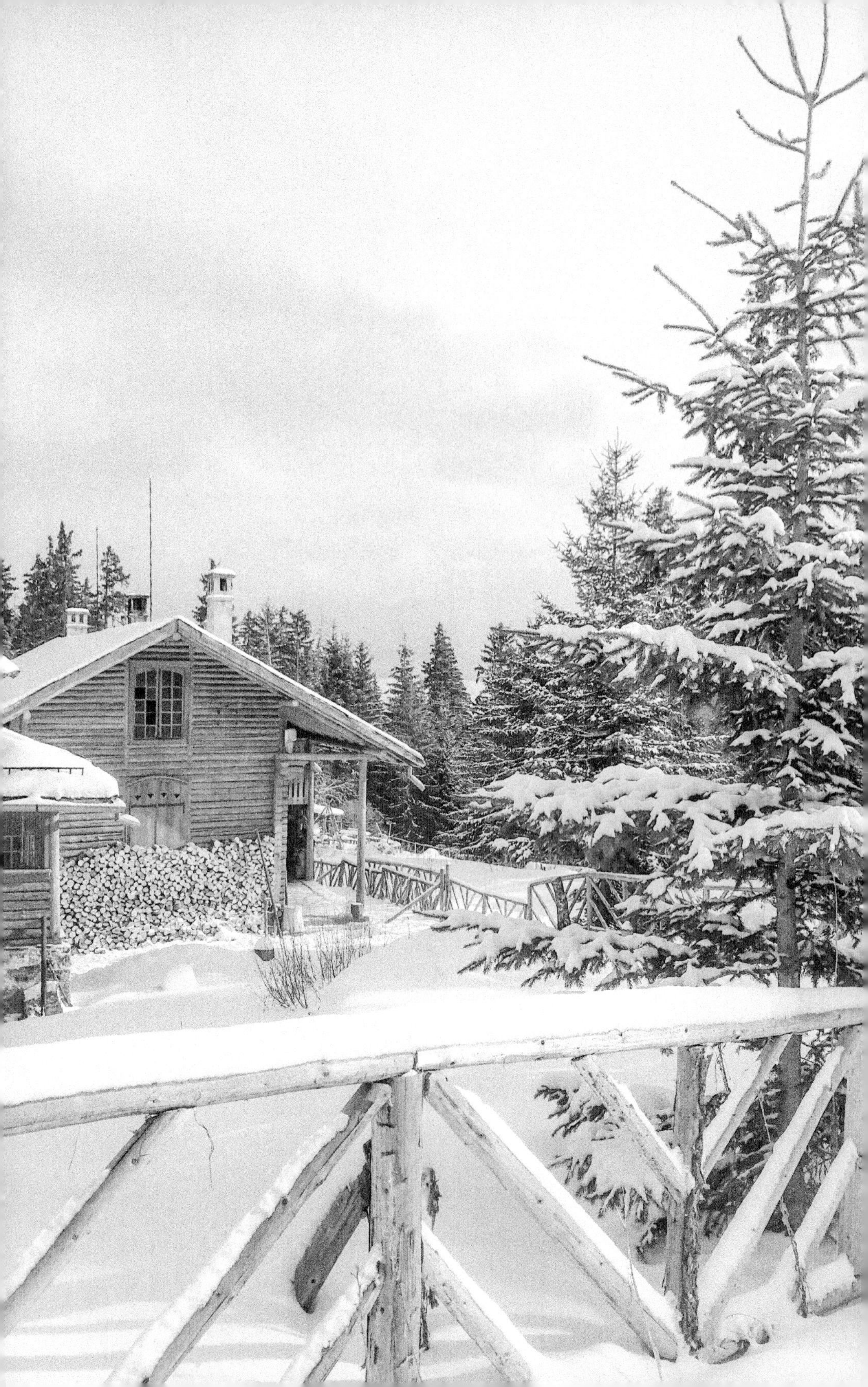

TITLE OF YOUR TRIP...

GET READY TO BECOME A STORY TELLER...

ADVENTURE YEARLY OVERVIEW

TRIPS TO PLAN & WHEN

Jan	Feb	Mar
Apr	May	Jun
Jul	Aug	Sep
Oct	Nov	Dec

INITIAL IDEAS

JOT ALL OF YOUR IDEAS, PLANS AND VISIONS FOR THE TRIP HERE

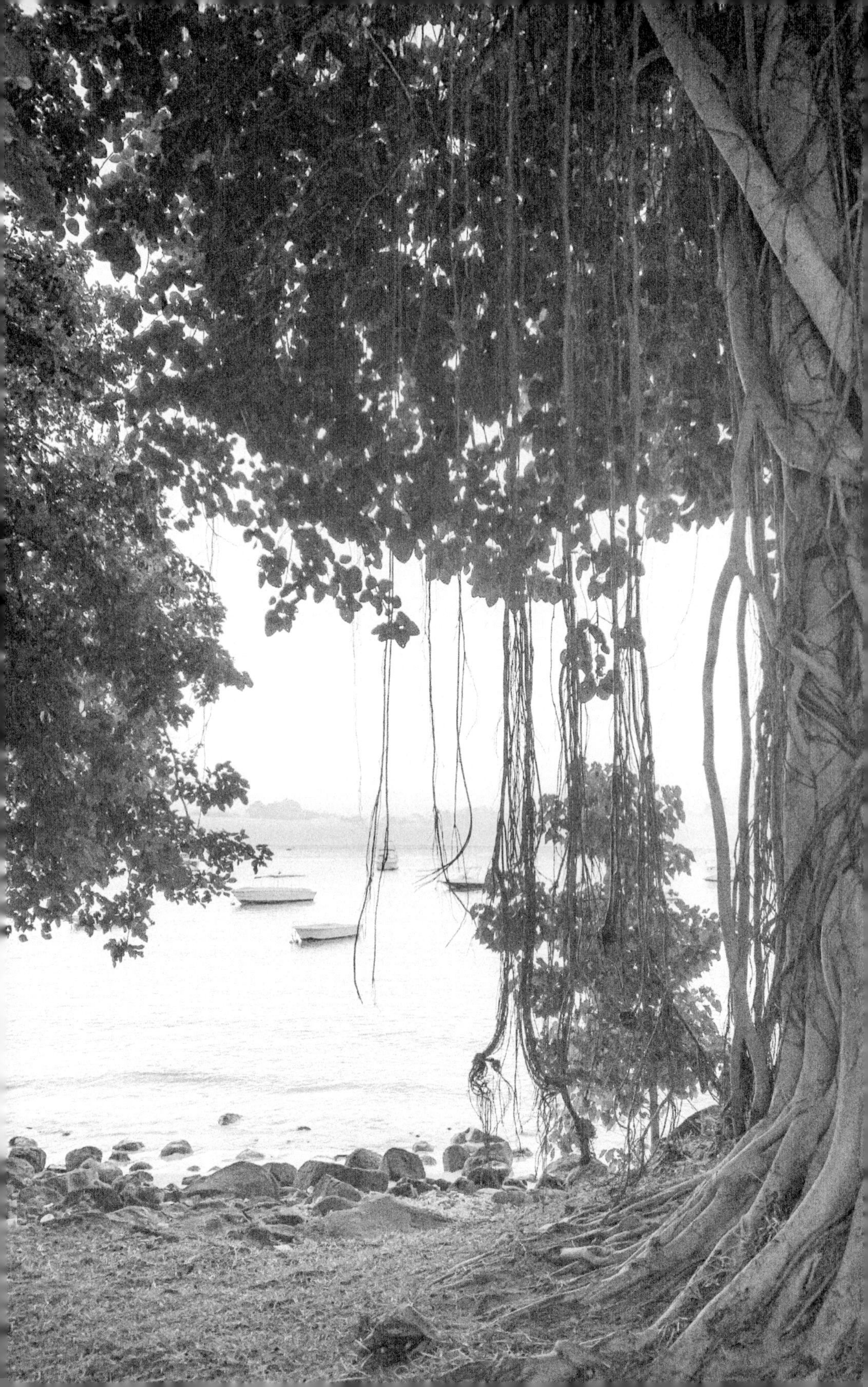

PLACES TO VISIT/ATTRACTIONS

(MUST SEE/DO EXPERIENCES I.E. HIKES/TRAILS, RESTAURANT, BEACHES/LAKES, EXCURSIONS)

PLACES TO VISIT	LOCATION	WHEN

PLACES TO VISIT	LOCATION	WHEN

PLACES TO VISIT/ATTRACTIONS

(MUST SEE/DO EXPERIENCES I.E. HIKES/TRAILS, RESTAURANT, BEACHES/LAKES, EXCURSIONS)

PLACES TO VISIT	LOCATION	WHEN

PLACES TO VISIT	LOCATION	WHEN

ITINERARY & PLANS

ACTIVITIES/PLANS	DATES	TIMES

ITINERARY & PLANS

ACTIVITIES/PLANS	DATES	TIMES

MONTHLY OVERVIEW

NOTE HERE KEY DATE REMINDERS FOR TRAVEL DATES, WHERE YOU WILL BE, APPOINTMENTS, DESTINATION STOPS ETC

MONTH: _____

MON	TUE	WED	THU	FRI	SAT	SUN

BUDGET PLANNING

ALLOCATE HOW MUCH MONEY YOU'LL NEED FOR EACH

PROVISIONS

FOOD	DRINKS	EATING OUT

BEING A TOURIST

EXCURSIONS	TRANSPORT	DINNER

TRAVEL

MISCELLANEOUS	FUEL	HIRE CAR

OTHER

SPENDING MONEY	MISCELLANEOUS	EMERGENCY

SAVINGS TRACKER

SAVING FOR: _____

GOAL AMOUNT: _____   DEADLINE: _____

DETAILS OF MONEY SAVED	AMOUNT	TOTAL SAVED

GETTING ORGANISED
- PACKING

WHAT TO PACK

CLOTHES

ACCESSORIES

SPECIALIST EQUIPMENT

FOOD/SUPPLIES

GETTING ORGANISED - ENTERTAINMENT

TRAVEL & RECREATIONAL ENTERTAINMENT

PLAYLISTS

PODCASTS

BOOKS & READING MATERIALS

CONSOLES/TECHNOLOGY ELECTRONICS

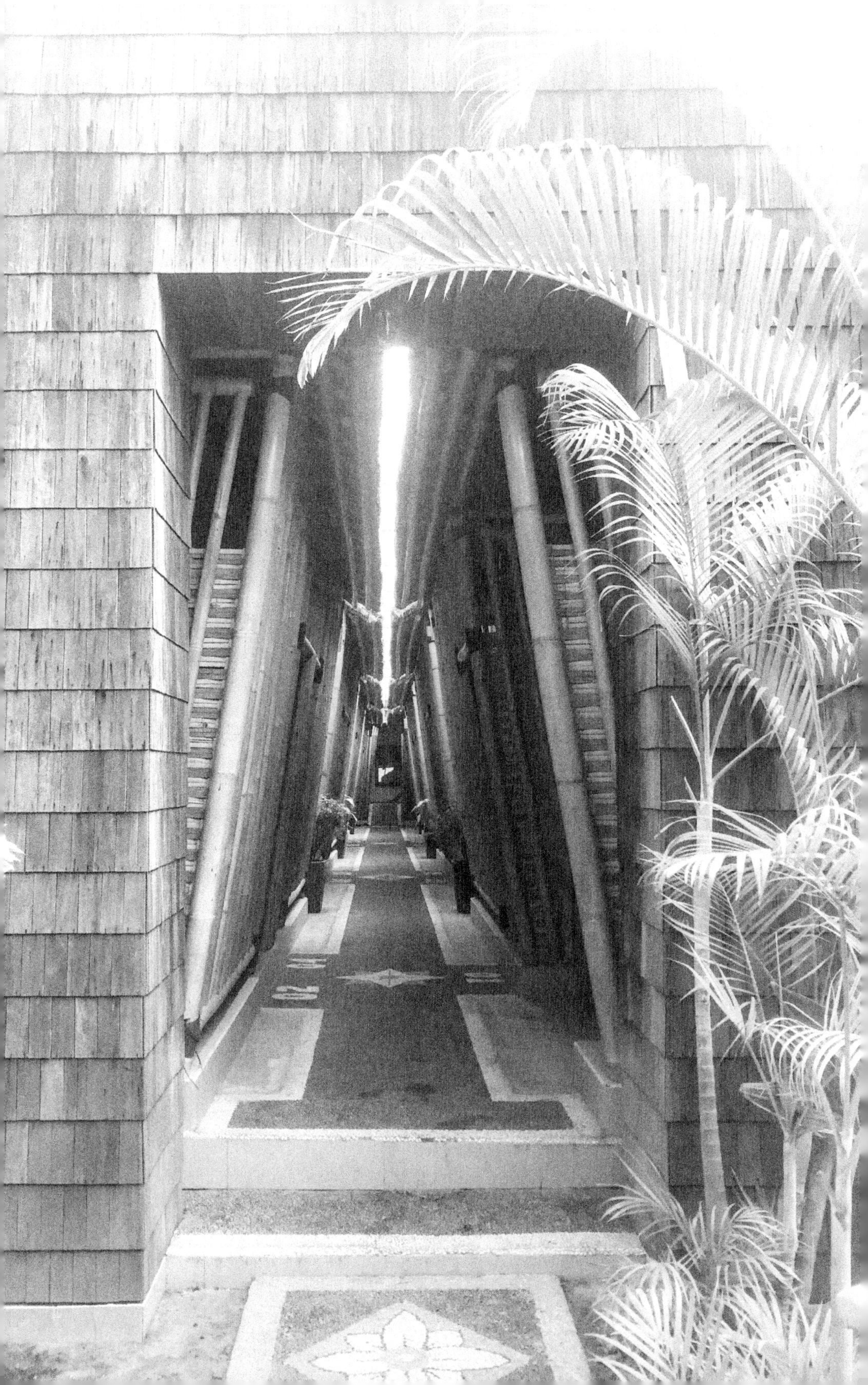

ACCOMMODATION

NAME OF ACCOMMODATION:

ADDRESS	LENGTH OF STAY	SCORE OUT OF 10

REVIEW/EXPERIENCE OF STAY

STAY AGAIN? ☐ YES ☐ NO

NAME OF ACCOMMODATION:

ADDRESS	LENGTH OF STAY	SCORE OUT OF 10

REVIEW/EXPERIENCE OF STAY

STAY AGAIN? ☐ YES ☐ NO

ACCOMMODATION

NAME OF ACCOMMODATION:

| ADDRESS | LENGTH OF STAY | SCORE OUT OF 10 |

REVIEW/EXPERIENCE OF STAY

STAY AGAIN?   ☐ YES   ☐ NO

NAME OF ACCOMMODATION:

| ADDRESS | LENGTH OF STAY | SCORE OUT OF 10 |

REVIEW/EXPERIENCE OF STAY

STAY AGAIN?   ☐ YES   ☐ NO

TRIP BUDGET TRACKER

BUDGET TOTAL

MONEY SPENT ON	AMOUNT	REMAINING

TRIP BUDGET TRACKER

CARRIED OVER

MONEY SPENT ON	AMOUNT	REMAINING

LOCAL BUSINESSES

NAME OF BUSINESS:		
ADDRESS	CONTACT NO	DETAILS

NAME OF BUSINESS:		
ADDRESS	CONTACT NO	DETAILS

NAME OF BUSINESS:		
ADDRESS	CONTACT NO	DETAILS

NAME OF BUSINESS:		
ADDRESS	CONTACT NO	DETAILS

LOCAL BUSINESSES

NAME OF BUSINESS:

| ADDRESS | CONTACT NO | DETAILS |

NAME OF BUSINESS:

| ADDRESS | CONTACT NO | DETAILS |

NAME OF BUSINESS:

| ADDRESS | CONTACT NO | DETAILS |

NAME OF BUSINESS:

| ADDRESS | CONTACT NO | DETAILS |

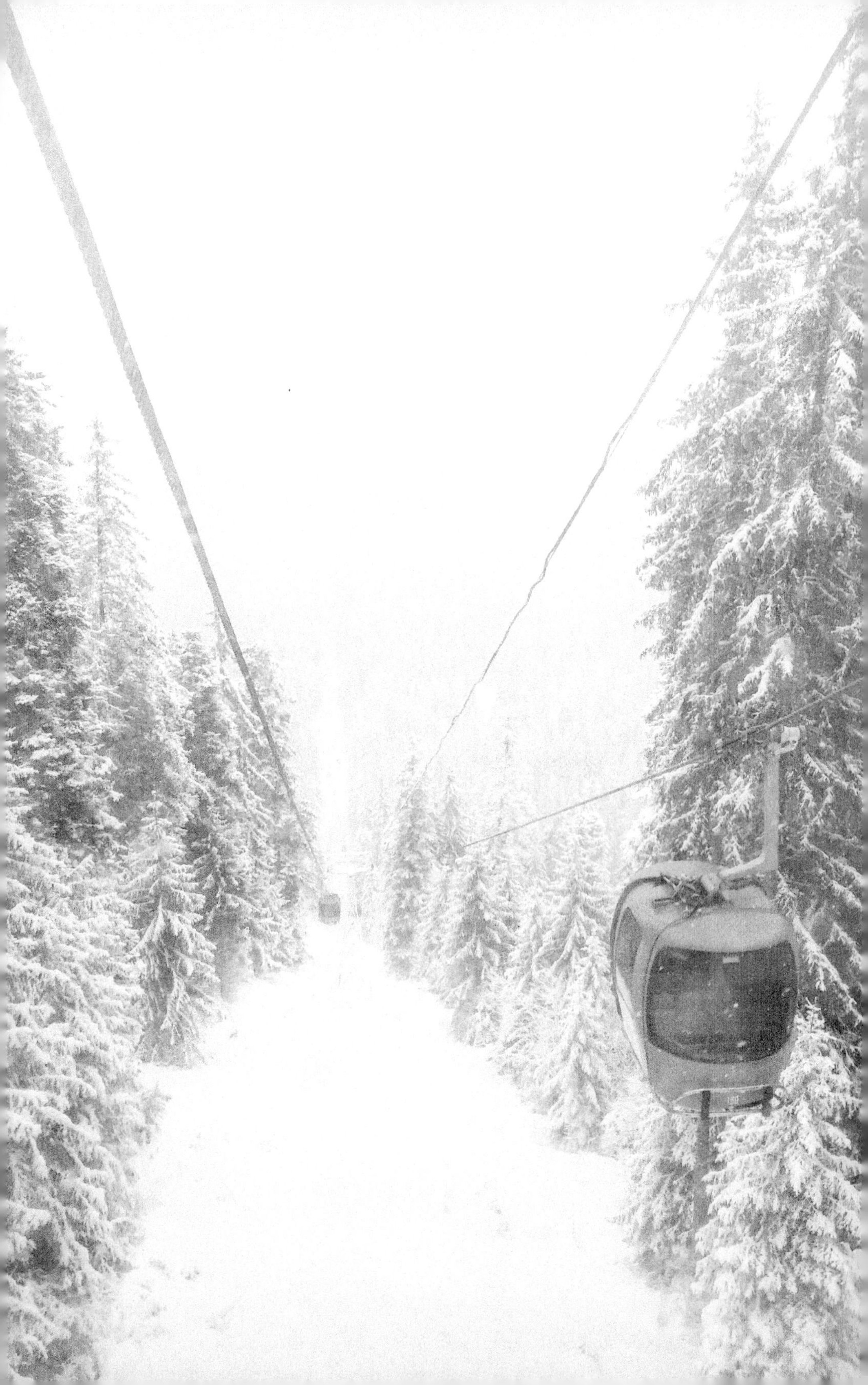

TRAVEL & TRANSPORT

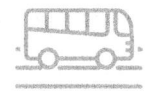

MODES OF TRANSPORT **DATES** **TIMES**

TRAVEL & TRANSPORT

| MODES OF TRANSPORT | DATES | TIMES |

OTHER IMPORTANT TRAVEL INFO & ROUTE MAPPING

JOURNEYS & ROUTES

TRAVEL INFO & ROUTE MAPPING

TRAVEL INFO & ROUTE MAPPING

DOODLES, DRAWINGS & IDEAS

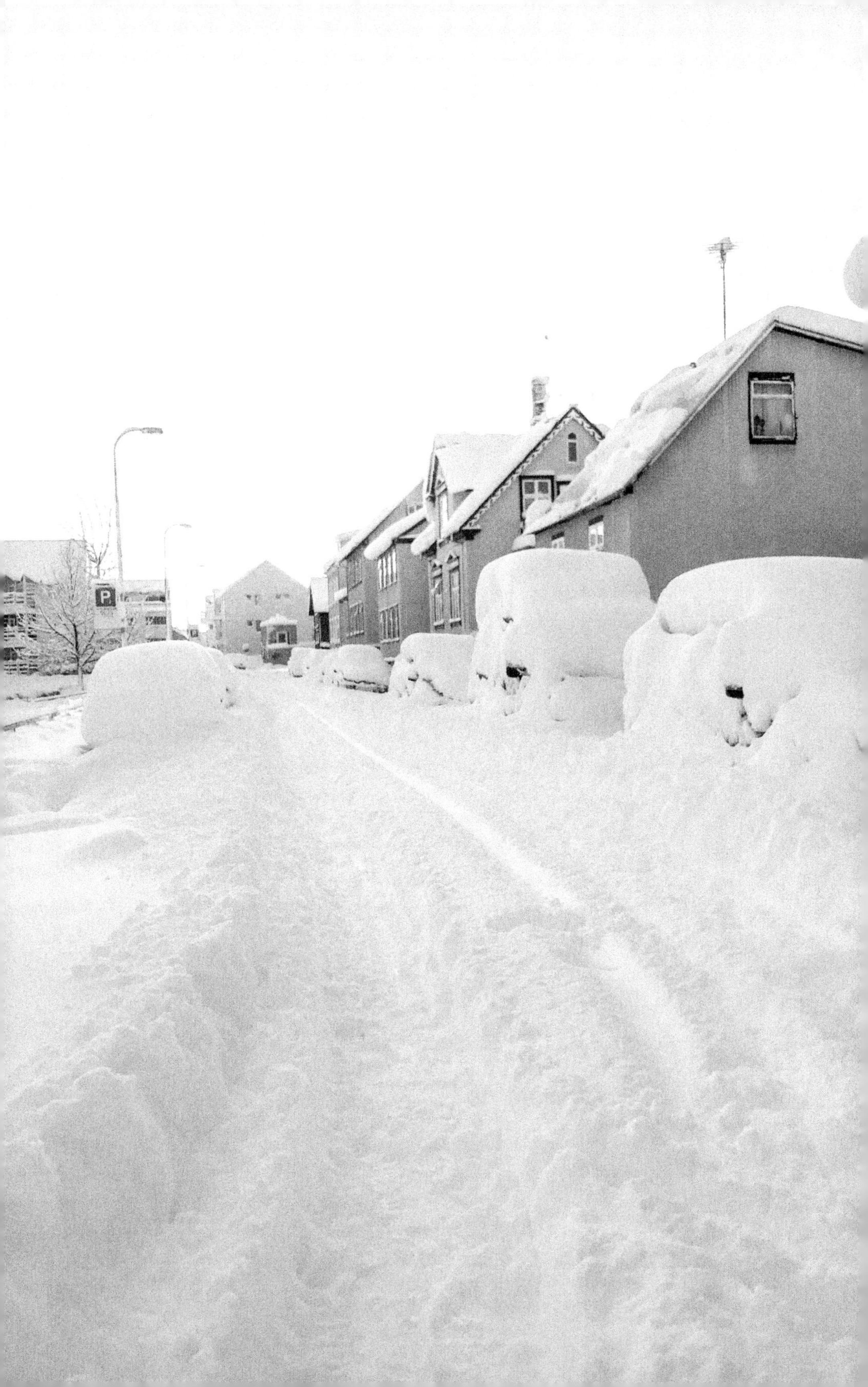
P

MEMORIES – PLACES VISITED

DESTINATION:

WHAT I SAW, ATE, FELT, EXPERIENCED, PEOPLE MET

FUNNY OR KEY MOMENTS TO REMEMBER

WHAT I'LL TAKE AWAY FROM THE EXPERIENCE

JOURNAL

MEMORIES – PLACES VISITED

DESTINATION:

WHAT I SAW, ATE, FELT, EXPERIENCED, PEOPLE MET

FUNNY OR KEY MOMENTS TO REMEMBER

WHAT I'LL TAKE AWAY FROM THE EXPERIENCE

JOURNAL

MEMORIES – PLACES VISITED

DESTINATION:

WHAT I SAW, ATE, FELT, EXPERIENCED, PEOPLE MET

FUNNY OR KEY MOMENTS TO REMEMBER

WHAT I'LL TAKE AWAY FROM THE EXPERIENCE

JOURNAL

MEMORIES - PLACES VISITED

DESTINATION:

WHAT I SAW, ATE, FELT, EXPERIENCED, PEOPLE MET

FUNNY OR KEY MOMENTS TO REMEMBER

WHAT I'LL TAKE AWAY FROM THE EXPERIENCE

JOURNAL

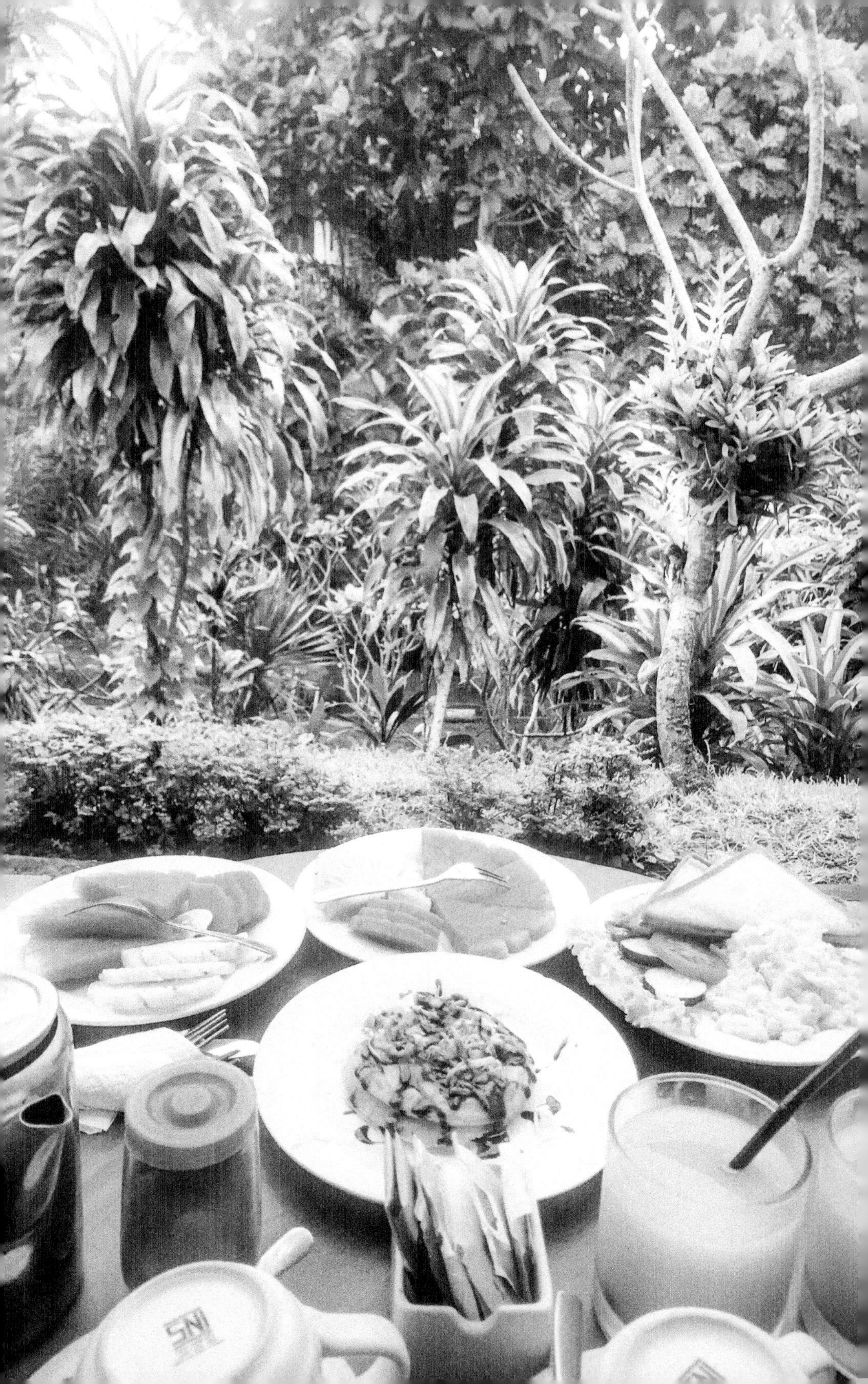

PLACE YOUR MEMORIES

STICK PHOTOS, TICKETS, MAPS

PLACE YOUR MEMORIES

STICK PHOTOS, TICKETS, MAPS

PLACE YOUR MEMORIES

STICK PHOTOS, TICKETS, MAPS

PLACE YOUR MEMORIES

STICK PHOTOS, TICKETS, MAPS

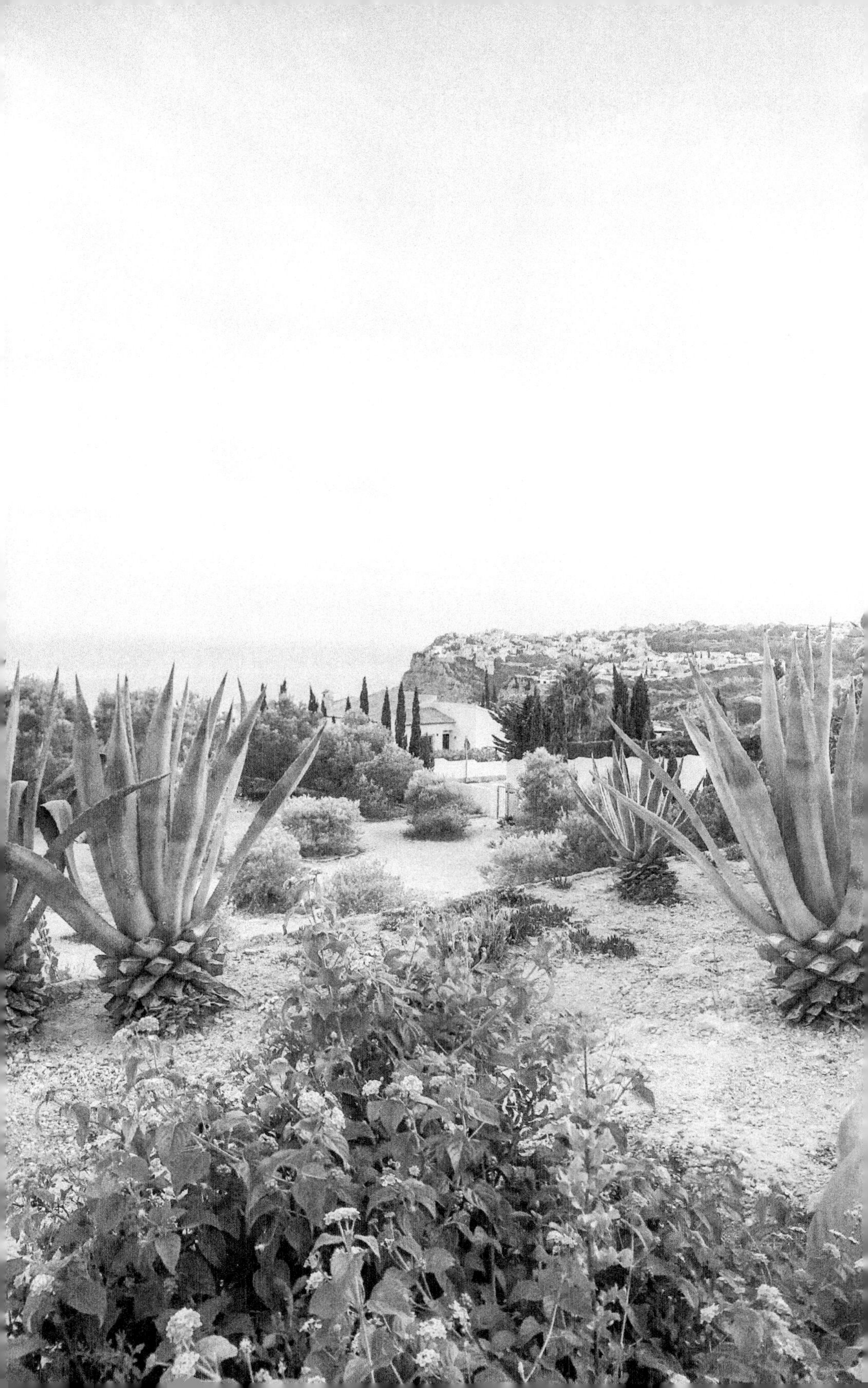

REFLECTION

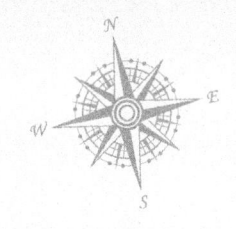

WHAT I'D DO DIFFERENTLY NEXT TIME

THINGS I'VE LEARNT

ADVICE I'D GIVE TO OTHERS

NOTES

NOTES

NOTES

NOTES

NOTES

NOTES

NOTES

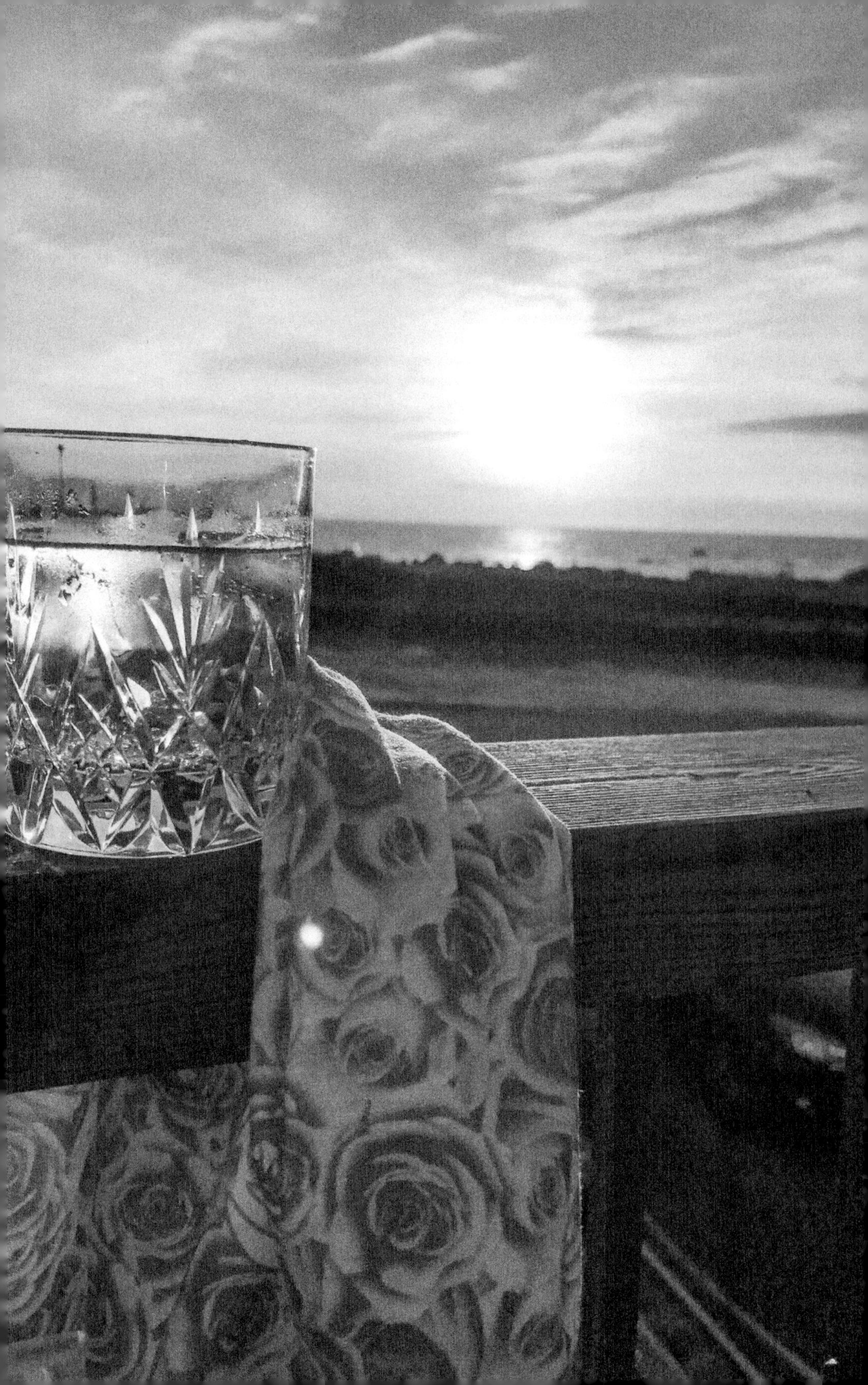

TITLE OF YOUR TRIP...

GET READY TO BECOME A STORY TELLER...

ADVENTURE YEARLY OVERVIEW

TRIPS TO PLAN & WHEN

Jan

Feb

Mar

Apr

May

Jun

Jul

Aug

Sep

Oct

Nov

Dec

INITIAL IDEAS

JOT ALL OF YOUR IDEAS, PLANS AND VISIONS FOR THE TRIP HERE

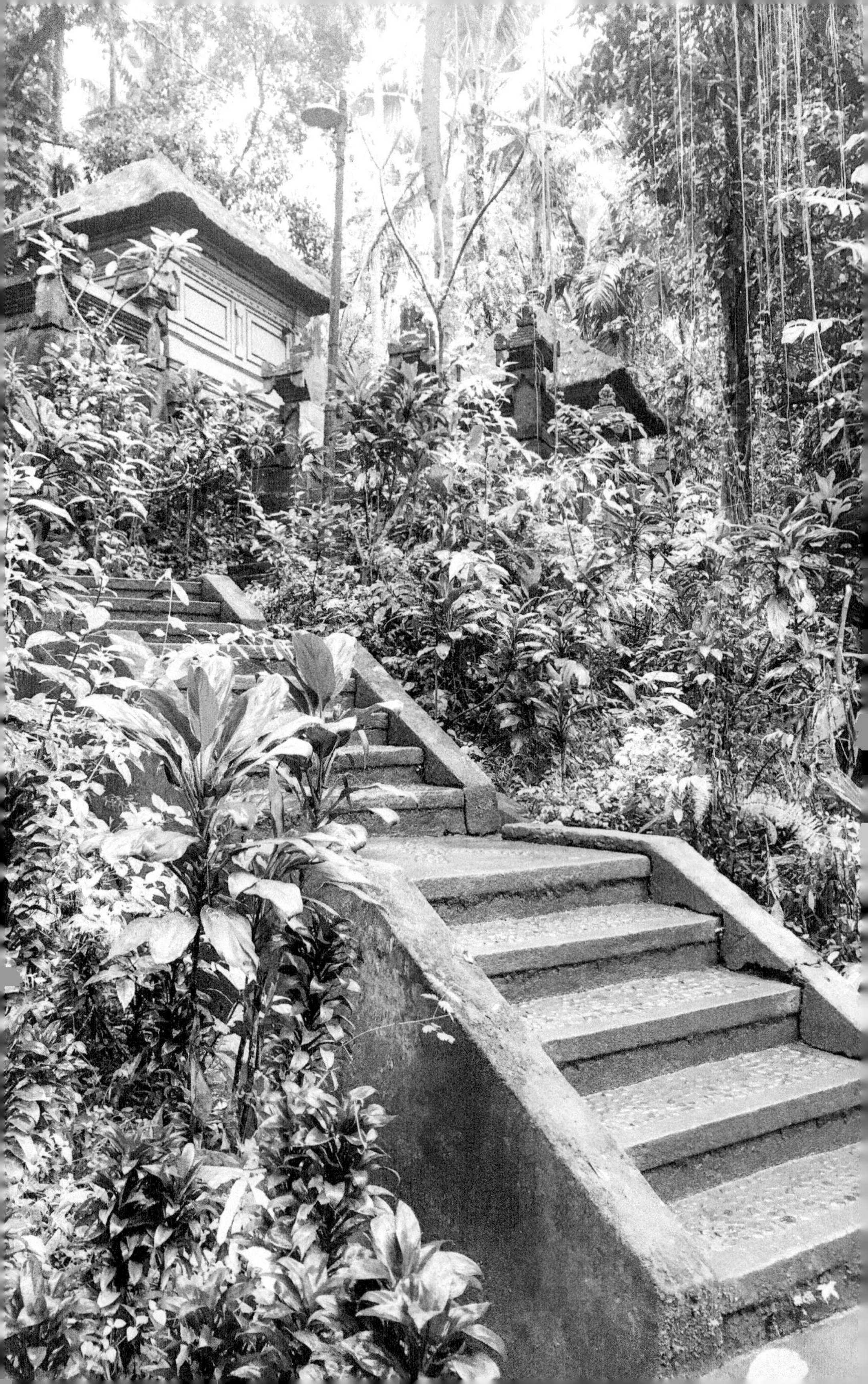

PLACES TO VISIT/ATTRACTIONS
(MUST SEE/DO EXPERIENCES I.E. HIKES/TRAILS, RESTAURANT, BEACHES/LAKES, EXCURSIONS)

PLACES TO VISIT	LOCATION	WHEN

PLACES TO VISIT	LOCATION	WHEN

PLACES TO VISIT/ATTRACTIONS

(MUST SEE/DO EXPERIENCES I.E. HIKES/TRAILS, RESTAURANT, BEACHES/LAKES, EXCURSIONS)

PLACES TO VISIT	LOCATION	WHEN

PLACES TO VISIT	LOCATION	WHEN

ITINERARY & PLANS

ACTIVITIES/PLANS	DATES	TIMES

ITINERARY & PLANS

ACTIVITIES/PLANS	DATES	TIMES

MONTHLY OVERVIEW

NOTE HERE KEY DATE REMINDERS FOR TRAVEL DATES, WHERE YOU WILL BE, APPOINTMENTS, DESTINATION STOPS ETC

MONTH: _____

MON	TUE	WED	THU	FRI	SAT	SUN

BUDGET PLANNING

ALLOCATE HOW MUCH MONEY YOU'LL NEED FOR EACH

PROVISIONS

FOOD	DRINKS	EATING OUT

BEING A TOURIST

EXCURSIONS	TRANSPORT	DINNER

TRAVEL

MISCELLANEOUS	FUEL	HIRE CAR

OTHER

SPENDING MONEY	MISCELLANEOUS	EMERGENCY

SAVINGS TRACKER

SAVING FOR: _____

GOAL AMOUNT: _____   DEADLINE: _____

DETAILS OF MONEY SAVED	AMOUNT	TOTAL SAVED

GETTING ORGANISED – PACKING

WHAT TO PACK

CLOTHES

ACCESSORIES

SPECIALIST EQUIPMENT

FOOD/SUPPLIES

GETTING ORGANISED
– ENTERTAINMENT

TRAVEL & RECREATIONAL ENTERTAINMENT

PLAYLISTS

PODCASTS

BOOKS & READING MATERIALS

CONSOLES/TECHNOLOGY ELECTRONICS

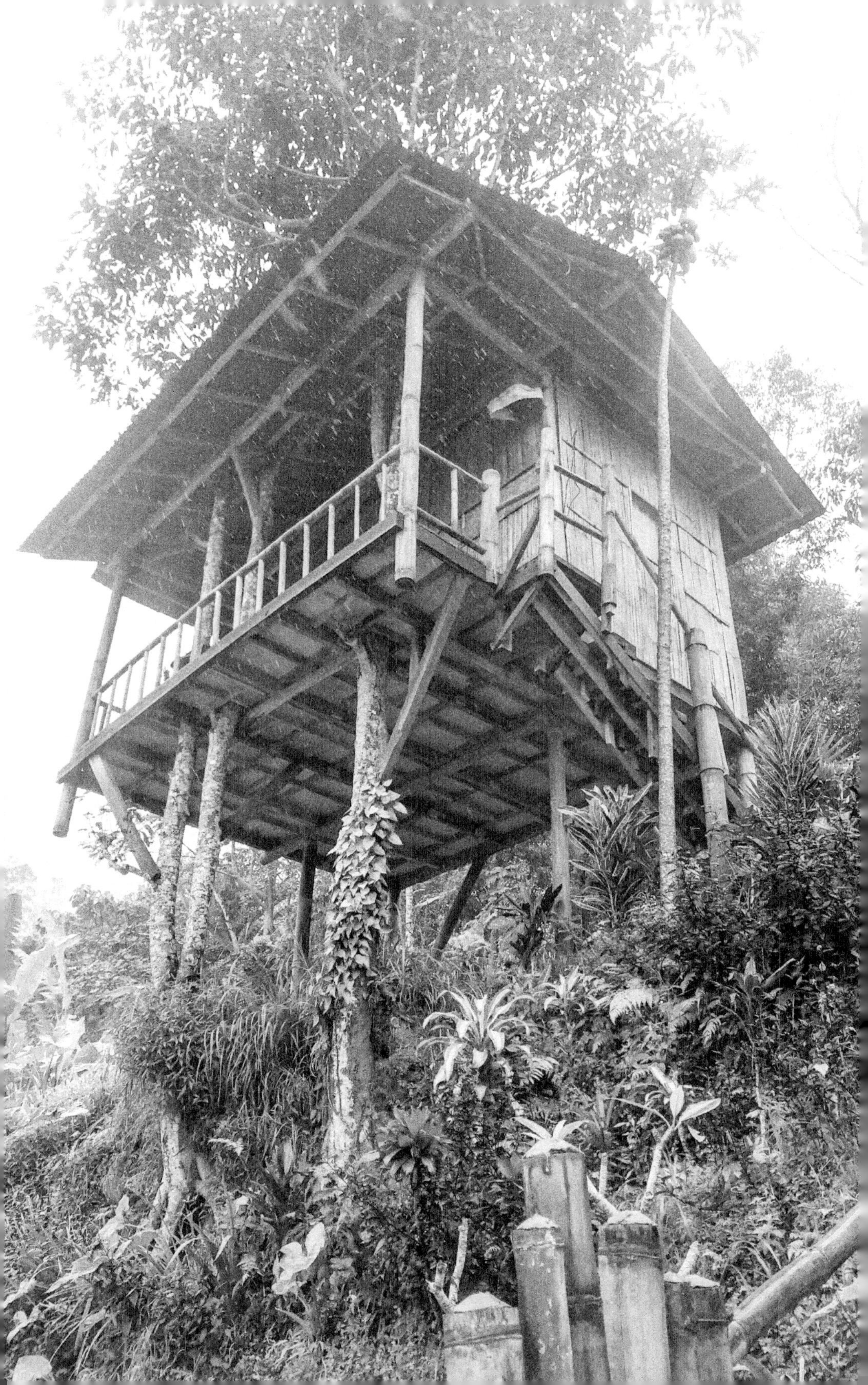

ACCOMMODATION

NAME OF ACCOMMODATION:

ADDRESS	LENGTH OF STAY	SCORE OUT OF 10

REVIEW/EXPERIENCE OF STAY

STAY AGAIN?   ☐ YES   ☐ NO

NAME OF ACCOMMODATION:

ADDRESS	LENGTH OF STAY	SCORE OUT OF 10

REVIEW/EXPERIENCE OF STAY

STAY AGAIN?   ☐ YES   ☐ NO

ACCOMMODATION

NAME OF ACCOMMODATION:

ADDRESS	LENGTH OF STAY	SCORE OUT OF 10

REVIEW/EXPERIENCE OF STAY

STAY AGAIN? ☐ YES ☐ NO

NAME OF ACCOMMODATION:

ADDRESS	LENGTH OF STAY	SCORE OUT OF 10

REVIEW/EXPERIENCE OF STAY

STAY AGAIN? ☐ YES ☐ NO

TRIP BUDGET TRACKER

BUDGET TOTAL

MONEY SPENT ON	AMOUNT	REMAINING

TRIP BUDGET TRACKER

CARRIED OVER

MONEY SPENT ON	AMOUNT	REMAINING

LOCAL BUSINESSES

NAME OF BUSINESS:

ADDRESS	CONTACT NO	DETAILS

NAME OF BUSINESS:

ADDRESS	CONTACT NO	DETAILS

NAME OF BUSINESS:

ADDRESS	CONTACT NO	DETAILS

NAME OF BUSINESS:

ADDRESS	CONTACT NO	DETAILS

LOCAL BUSINESSES

NAME OF BUSINESS:		
ADDRESS	CONTACT NO	DETAILS

NAME OF BUSINESS:		
ADDRESS	CONTACT NO	DETAILS

NAME OF BUSINESS:		
ADDRESS	CONTACT NO	DETAILS

NAME OF BUSINESS:		
ADDRESS	CONTACT NO	DETAILS

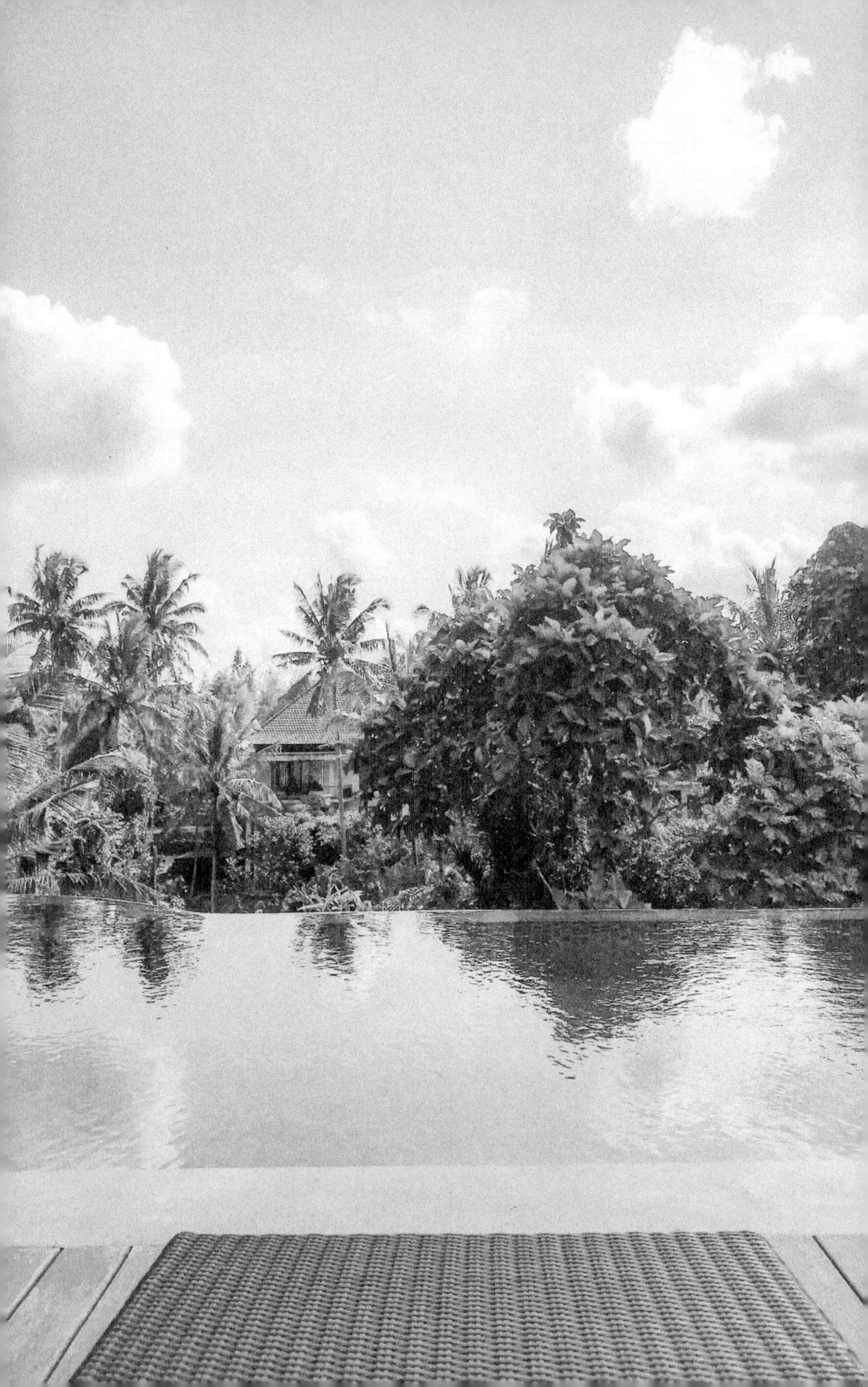

TRAVEL & TRANSPORT

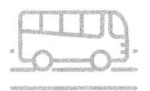

MODES OF TRANSPORT **DATES** **TIMES**

TRAVEL & TRANSPORT

MODES OF TRANSPORT **DATES** **TIMES**

OTHER IMPORTANT TRAVEL INFO & ROUTE MAPPING

JOURNEYS & ROUTES

TRAVEL INFO & ROUTE MAPPING

TRAVEL INFO & ROUTE MAPPING

DOODLES, DRAWINGS & IDEAS

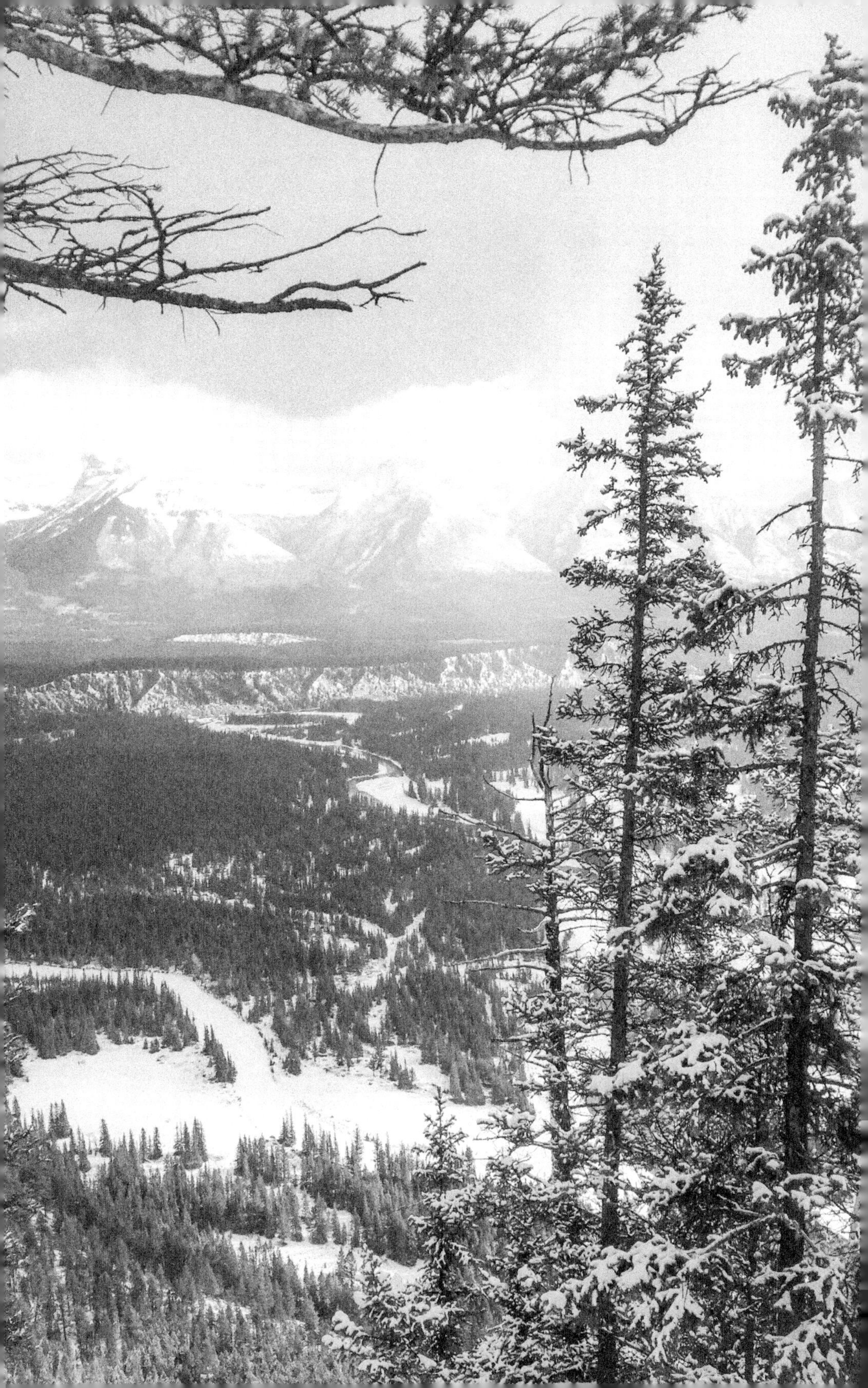

MEMORIES - PLACES VISITED

DESTINATION:

WHAT I SAW, ATE, FELT, EXPERIENCED, PEOPLE MET

FUNNY OR KEY MOMENTS TO REMEMBER

WHAT I'LL TAKE AWAY FROM THE EXPERIENCE

JOURNAL

MEMORIES - PLACES VISITED

DESTINATION:

WHAT I SAW, ATE, FELT, EXPERIENCED, PEOPLE MET

FUNNY OR KEY MOMENTS TO REMEMBER

WHAT I'LL TAKE AWAY FROM THE EXPERIENCE

JOURNAL

MEMORIES – PLACES VISITED

DESTINATION:

WHAT I SAW, ATE, FELT, EXPERIENCED, PEOPLE MET

FUNNY OR KEY MOMENTS TO REMEMBER

WHAT I'LL TAKE AWAY FROM THE EXPERIENCE

JOURNAL

MEMORIES - PLACES VISITED

DESTINATION:

WHAT I SAW, ATE, FELT, EXPERIENCED, PEOPLE MET

FUNNY OR KEY MOMENTS TO REMEMBER

WHAT I'LL TAKE AWAY FROM THE EXPERIENCE

JOURNAL

PLACE YOUR MEMORIES

STICK PHOTOS, TICKETS, MAPS

PLACE YOUR MEMORIES

STICK PHOTOS, TICKETS, MAPS

PLACE YOUR MEMORIES

STICK PHOTOS, TICKETS, MAPS

PLACE YOUR MEMORIES

STICK PHOTOS, TICKETS, MAPS

REFLECTION

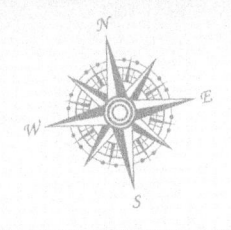

WHAT I'D DO DIFFERENTLY NEXT TIME

THINGS I'VE LEARNT

ADVICE I'D GIVE TO OTHERS

NOTES

NOTES

NOTES

NOTES

NOTES

NOTES

NOTES

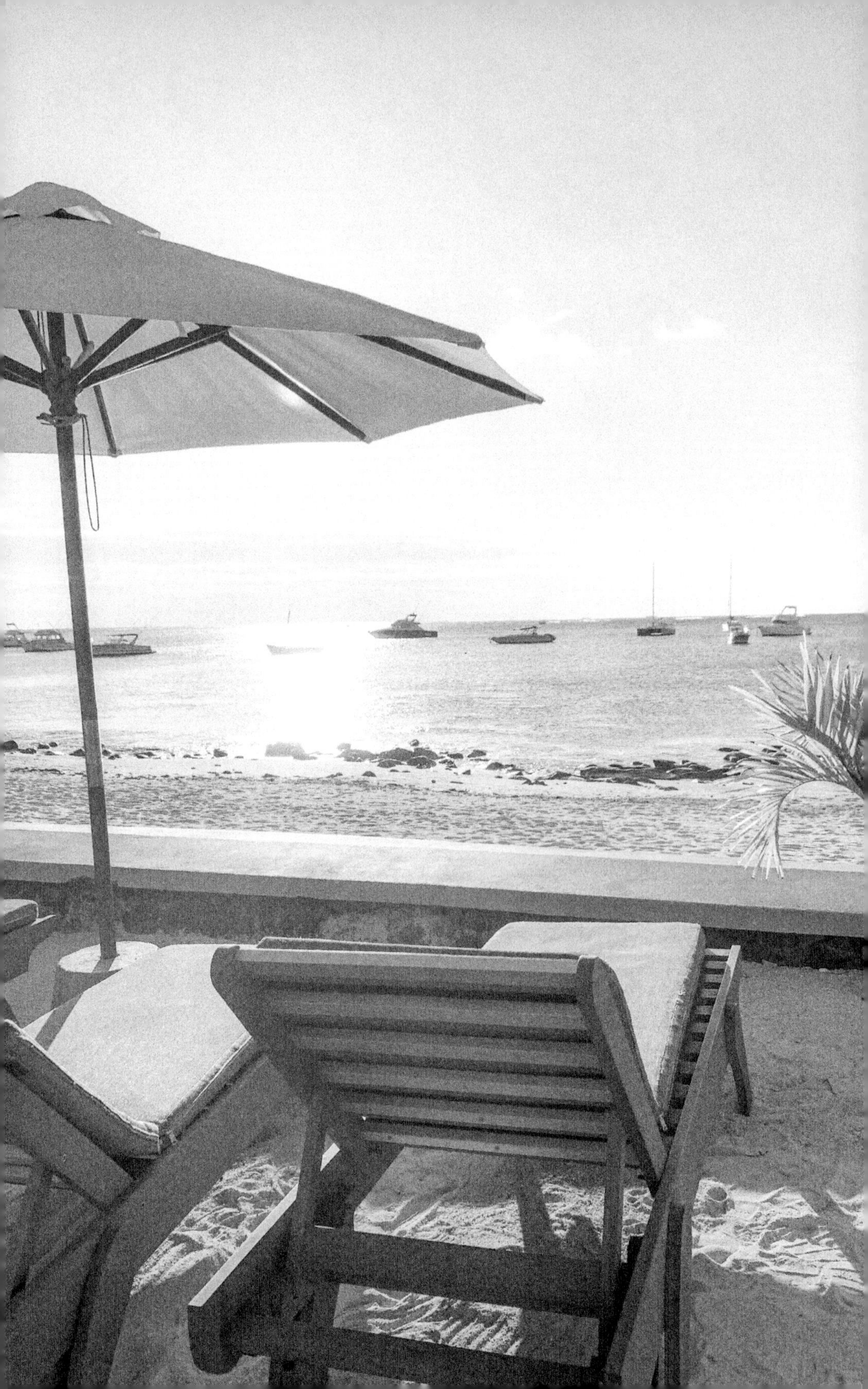

Printed in Great Britain
by Amazon